St Faustina

APOSTLE OF DIVINE MERCY

Compiled and introduced by
Don Mullan

First published in 2005 by
The Columba Press
55A Spruce Avenue, Stillorgan Industrial Park,
Blackrock, Co Dublin

Designed by Bill Bolger
Origination by The Columba Press
Printed in Ireland by
Betaprint, Dublin

ISBN 1 85607 492 7

Compilation copyright © 2005, Don Mullan

With gratitude to
Patrick and Carmel Walshe

and to

Matt and Mary Long
dear friends of the late
Gabriel (Gary) Burke

Acknowledgements

The publisher and editor gratefully acknowledge the permission to the following to quote from material in their copyright: Congregation of Marians of the Immaculate Conception, Stockbridge, MA 01263, for quotations from: *Diary – Divine Mercy in My Soul* by Saint Maria Faustina Kowalska, © 1987.
Web: http://www.marian.org

Author's Acknowledgements

Sincere thanks are owed to the following for their invaluable support and assistance with this publication:

Patrick and Carmel Walshe for their trust, support and immense kindness. They made it possible for me to find time to research and compile this little book, which included a wonderful visit to Krakow in April 2005, thus enabling me to deepen my understanding of St Faustina Kowalska and her revelations of Divine Mercy. Thanks are also extended to Patrick O'Neill Smyth who hosted our visit to Krakow and who arranged my meeting with the Polish Sisters of Our Lady of Mercy. I am especially grateful to Sr Diane, one of the sisters who welcome English-speaking pilgrims, for her precious time, knowledge and insights at the Chapel and Shrine of Divine Mercy, Lagiewniki, Krakow. It was there that I made the final selection of quotations that appear in this little book. I am also deeply grateful to Val Conlon of Divine Mercy Publications, Ireland, for the time and guidance he too offered me. I am especially grateful to my mother-in-law, Maureen Beatty, who introduced me to the diary of St Faustina, from which all of the quotations are taken, and to my sister, Moya Mullan, for her guidance and advice. Thanks also to Yvonne Golding for secretarial support; to Seamus Cashman who planted the seed of this Little Book series. Finally, loving thanks to my family, Margaret, Thérèse, Carl and Emma, for their continued patience, understanding, kindness and warmth.

INTRODUCTION

Pope John Paul II, in his book, *Memory & Identity – Personal Reflections*, (Weidenfeld & Nicholson, London 2005), refers to St Maria Faustina Kowalska as 'chosen by Christ to be a particularly enlightened interpreter of the truth of Divine Mercy.' He expressed astonishment at the profundity of her mystical revelations, as contained in her Diary, despite the fact that she was a simple and uneducated person.

Reflecting on the dual influences of the ideologies of Nazism and Communism throughout the 20th century, John Paul II wrote that Saint Faustina Heralded a message capable of counteracting the immorality contained in both ideologies, particularly the truth that the merciful Jesus reflects the God of Mercy. Because of this he felt urged, when he became Pope, to share with the universal church Sister Faustina's experiences.

Pope John Paul II became the greatest advocate of Sr Faustina's apostolate. During his pontificate devotion to Divine Mercy began to find its way into almost every Catholic diocese and parish throughout the world. It was he who fulfilled the mystical request made to the saint by Christ of establishing the first Sunday after Easter as the Feast of Divine Mercy. Many believe it providential that his death on Saturday, 2 April 2005, occurred during the vigil of this Feast. This resulted in many global media networks reporting the reaction of the Polish people to his death from the Shrine of Divine Mercy.

This little book has attempted to focus on the deep personal spirituality of St Faustina. I have, therefore, deliberately decided to concentrate primarily on her own words and not those spoken to her during her mystical experiences by both Christ and, on occasions, the Blessed Mother. I made the following selection of quotations at the Shrine of Divine Mercy on 29 April 2005. It is hoped that the reader will discover that despite her lack of education, Sr Faustina's simple life of prayer, devotion and works of Mercy led her to discover a profound depth of spiritual wisdom that is the gift of the Holy Spirit.

St Maria Faustina was born Helena

Kowalska, the third of ten children, in Glogowiec, Poland, on 25 August 1905, of a poor and religious family. At 19 she entered the Congregation of the Sisters of Our Lady of Mercy, having spent three years working as a housekeeper. Her spirituality was grounded in her love of the Eucharist, devotion to the Mother of Mercy and compassion for the poor, the sick and the dying. Having been consumed by tuberculosis and innumerable sufferings, borne with serenity and abandonment, she died in Krakow on 5 October 1938. She was canonised by Pope John Paul II on the Feast of Divine Mercy,

30 April 2000. Her remains rest at the Sanctuary of Divine Mercy, Krakow-Lagiewniki, Poland.

Don Mullan
Dublin, Ireland
25 August 2005

Quotations from St Faustina
APOSTLE OF DIVINE MERCY

The Fountain of Mercy

Jesus … told me … that these words
must be clearly in evidence:
'Jesus, I trust in you.'

I am offering people a vessel
with which they are to keep coming
for graces to the fountain of mercy.
That vessel is [the] image of Divine
Mercy with the signature
'Jesus I trust in you.'
(327)

Trust

Then I heard a voice:

**The graces of my mercy
are drawn by means of one vessel
only, and that is – trust.
The more a soul trusts,
the more it will receive.
(1567/1578)**

THE DIVINE-HUMAN HEART

On Friday during Mass
when my soul was flooded
with God's happiness,
I heard these words in my soul:

**My mercy has passed into souls
through the divine-human heart
of Jesus as a ray from the sun
passes through crystal. (528)**

Unfathomable Mercy

I know that … [some] souls …
well-advanced in the … spiritual life
do not have the courage
to entrust themselves completely to God
… [T]his is … because few souls know
the unfathomable mercy of God
and his great goodness. (731)

Exercising Mercy

O my Jesus, you yourself must help me …
You see how very little I am, and …
depend solely on your goodness:

I am giving you three ways of exercising mercy toward your neighbour - the first by deed, the second by word, the third by prayer. In these … is contained the fullness of mercy and it is an unquestionable proof of love for me. (742)

Full of Mercy

O my Jesus each of your saints reflects
one of your virtues; I desire to reflect
your compassionate heart, full of mercy;
I want to glorify it. Let your mercy,
O Jesus, be impressed upon my heart and
soul like a seal,
and this will be my badge in this
and the future life. (1242)

FOUNT OF MERCY

O Eternal Love, you command your
sacred image to be painted
and reveal to us
the inconceivable fount of mercy.
You bless whoever approaches your rays,
and a soul all black will turn into snow. (1)

Merciful Gaze

Eternal Father, turn your merciful gaze
upon the souls of those
who as yet do not know you,
but who are enclosed in
the most compassionate heart of Jesus.
Draw them to the light of the gospel.
These souls do not know
what great happiness it is to love you.

(1217)

THE SONG OF MERCY

With you, Jesus, I go through life,
amid storms and rainbows,
with a cry of joy,
singing the song of your mercy. (761)

FEAST OF DIVINE MERCY

How great is this work of the most high
God. I am but his instrument.
Oh, how ardently I desire to see
this Feast of the Divine Mercy
which God is demanding through me.
But if it is the will of God
that it be celebrated solemnly
only after my death,
even so I rejoice in it already. (711)

GOODNESS AND MERCY

Whatever Jesus did, he did well.
He went along, doing good.
His manner was full of goodness and mercy.
His steps were guided by compassion.
Toward his enemies he showed goodness,
kindness and understanding,
and to those in need help and consolation.

(1175)

That I May Be Merciful

Help me, O Lord,
that my eyes may be merciful,
so that I may never suspect
or judge from appearances,
but look for what is beautiful
in my neighbours' souls
and come to their rescue. (163)

THAT I MAY BE MERCIFUL

Help me, that my ears may be merciful,
so that I may give heed
to my neighbours' needs
and not be indifferent
to their pains and moanings. (163)

THAT I MAY BE MERCIFUL

Help me, O Lord,
that my tongue may be merciful,
so that I should never speak negatively
of my neighbour,
but have a word of comfort
and forgiveness for all. (163)

THAT I MAY BE MERCIFUL

Help me, O Lord,
that my hands may be merciful
and filled with good deeds,
so that I may do only good
to my neighbours and take upon myself
the more difficult and toilsome tasks.

(163)

That I May Be Merciful

Help me, that my feet may be merciful,
so that I may hurry
to assist my neighbour,
overcoming my own fatigue
and weariness.
My true rest is
in the service of my neighbour. (163)

THAT I MAY BE MERCIFUL

Help me, O Lord,
that my heart may be merciful
so that I myself may feel
all the sufferings of my neighbour.
I will refuse my heart to no one.
I will be sincere even with those who,
I know, will abuse my kindness. (163)

That I May Be Merciful

I ask you to make my heart so big
that there will be room in it
for the needs of all the souls
living on the face of the earth …
my love extends beyond the world,
to the souls suffering in purgatory…
O Jesus, make my heart sensitive
to all the sufferings of my neighbour,
whether of body or of soul.
O my Jesus, I know that you act toward us
as we act toward our neighbour. (692)

LOVE AND MERCY

… the greatest attribute is love and mercy.
It unites the creature with the Creator.
This immense love and abyss of mercy
are made known
in the incarnation of the Word
and in the redemption [of humanity].
(180)

Pure Love

I have come to know
that only love is of any value;
love is greatness;
nothing, no works,
can compare with
a single act of pure love of God. (1092)

Pure Love

Pure love is capable of great deeds,
and it is not broken by difficulty
or adversity …
It will not do anything
that might displease God …
The more it gives of itself,
the happier it is …
it knows how to unmask and
also knows with whom it has to deal.
(140)

Pure Love

In pure love,
there is room for everything… (947)

Love

Oh, with what inconceivable favours
God gifts a soul that loves him sincerely!
(778)

Love

Suddenly I saw the Lord
in his inexpressible beauty.
He looked at me graciously and said,

**My daughter,
I too came down from heaven
out of love for you.
I lived for you, I died for you,
and I created the heavens for you.
(853)**

THE LOVE OF GOD

The love of God makes a soul free. (890)

The Love of God

As long as we live,
the love of God grows in us.
Until we die,
we ought to strive for the love of God.
(1191)

Constant Love

Everything may change,
but love never, never;
it is always the same. (890)

Only Love

Only love has meaning;
it raises up our smallest actions
into infinity. (502)

SINCERE LOVE

If a soul loves God sincerely
and is intimately united with him,
then, even… in the midst of
difficult external circumstances,
nothing can disturb its interior life;
and in the midst of corruption,
it can remain pure and unsullied …
God … protects in a special way,
even in a miraculous way,
a soul that loves him sincerely. (1094)

GREAT LOVE

Jesus, you have given me to know
and understand
in what a soul's greatness consists:
not in great deeds but in great love. (889)

THE FLOWER OF LOVE

Mercy is the flower of love.
God is love, and mercy is his deed.
In love it is conceived;
in mercy it is revealed.
Everything I look at
speaks to me of God's mercy. (651)

A Person's Greatness

O my Jesus,
I know that a person's greatness
is evidenced by his deeds
and not by his words or feelings.
It is the works that have come from us
that will speak about us. (663)

FAITHFULNESS

I see clearly that no one can release me
from the duty of doing
the known will of God …
give me the grace
that I may always be faithful to you. (787)

FAITHFULNESS

My whole soul listens intently
to God's wishes.
I do always what God asks of me,
although my nature often quakes
and I feel that
the magnitude of these things
is beyond my strength. (652)

FAITHFULNESS

Wherever [God] puts me,
I will try faithfully to do his holy will …
even if the will of God
were to be as hard and difficult for me
as was the will of the heavenly Father
for his Son,
as he prayed in the Garden of Olives.

(1394)

Free Will

God never violates our free will.
It is up to us whether we want
to receive God's grace or not.
It is up to us whether
we will co-operate with it or waste it.

GRACE

Suddenly Jesus stood before me and said,
What are you doing here so early?
I answered, 'I am thinking of you,
of your mercy and your goodness
toward us. And you Jesus,
what are you doing here?'
**I have come out to meet you,
to lavish new graces on you.
I am looking for souls who would like
to receive my grace. (1705)**

GRACE

O my Jesus, how prone I am to evil
and this forces me
to be constantly vigilant.
But I do not loose heart.
I trust God's grace,
which abounds in the worst misery. (606)

GRACE

Sustained by your grace,
I am ready to follow you, Lord,
not only to Tabor,
but also to Calvary. (1488)

The Passion

… what will become of sinners
if they do not take advantage
of the passion of Jesus?
In his passion,
I see a whole sea of mercy. (948)

THE PASSION

This long illness
has sapped my strength completely.
I am uniting myself with Jesus
through suffering.
When I meditate on his painful passion,
my physical sufferings are lessened. (1625)

THE SUFFERING

When I feel that the suffering
is more than I can bear,
I take refuge in the Lord
in the Blessed Sacrament
and I speak to him with profound silence.

(73)

The Deep Night

O my Jesus, despite the deep night
that is all around me
and the dark clouds which hide the horizon,
I know that the sun never goes out.
O Lord, though I cannot comprehend you
and do not understand your ways,
I nonetheless trust in your mercy. (73)

On the Cross

Today the Lord said to me:
… the greater the misery of a soul,
the greater its right to my mercy;
[urge] all souls to trust in the
unfathomable abyss of my mercy,
because I want to save them all.
On the cross,
the fountain of my mercy was
opened wide by the lance for all souls
– no one have I excluded! (1182)

Darkness of the soul

Darkness of the soul …
The Lord has hidden himself
and I am alone, all alone …
Not a single ray of light
penetrates my soul.
I do not understand myself
or those who speak to me.
Frightful temptations
regarding the holy faith assail me …
O hurricane, what are you doing
to the boat of my heart? (1558)

Abandonment

My soul underwent
a complete abandonment
on the part of creatures;
often my best intentions
were misinterpreted …
a type of suffering that is most painful;
but God allows it and we must accept it
because in this way
we become more like Jesus. (38)

Illness

I made an hour of adoration
in thanksgiving for the grace
which had been granted me
and for my illness.
Illness also is a great grace.
I have been ill for four months,
but I do not recall having wasted
so much as a minute of it.
All has been for God and souls;
I want to be faithful to him everywhere.

(1062)

Illness

I thank God for this illness
and these physical discomforts,
because I have time to converse
with the Lord Jesus.
It is my delight to spend long hours
at the feet of the hidden God,
and the hours pass like minutes
as I lose track of time. (784)

Way of the Cross

When I make the Way of the Cross,
I am deeply moved at the twelfth station.
Here I reflect on
the omnipotence of God's mercy
which passed through the heart of Jesus.
In this open wound …
I enclose all poor humans…
and those individuals whom I love…
(1309)

Humility

O humility,
the most precious of virtues,
how few souls possess you! (1436)

HUMILITY

O humility, lovely flower,
I see how few souls possess you.
Is it because you are so beautiful
and at the same time
so difficult to attain? (1306)

Humility

I never cringe before anyone.
I can't bear flattery,
for humility is nothing but the truth.
There is no cringing in true humility …
Little matter that often I hear people say
that I am proud,
for I know that human judgement
does not discern the motives
for our actions. (1502)

Humility

I will hide from people's eyes
whatever good I am able to do
so that God himself may be my reward.
I will be like a tiny violet
hidden in the grass,
which does not hurt
the foot that treads on it,
but diffuses its fragrance … (255)

Humility

There will be no distinction
between the sisters, no mothers,
no reverends, no venerables,
but all will be equal,
even though there might be
great differences in their parentage.
We know who Jesus was
and yet how he humbled himself
and with whom he associated. (538)

Humility

Here are a few words from a conversation I had with the Mother Directress [Mary Joseph] toward the end of my novitiate:
'… Remember this, Sister,
for your whole life:
as waters flow from the mountains
down into the valleys,
so, too, do God's graces
flow only into humble souls.' (55)

The Blessed Mother

O Mary, you are joy,
because through you
God descended to earth
[and] into my heart. (40)

THE BLESSED MOTHER

The Blessed Mother was telling me
to accept all that God asked of me
like a little child, without questioning;
otherwise it would not be pleasing to God.
(529)

The Blessed Mother

The Blessed Virgin… instructed me…
*The soul's true greatness is in loving God
and in humbling oneself in his presence…
because the Lord is great,
but he is well-pleased only with the humble;
he always opposes the proud.* (1711)

THE BLESSED MOTHER

… I am fully resigned
to the will of God … I desire nothing
but the fulfillment of his holy will.
I am uniting myself with
the Mother of God
and I am leaving Nazareth
and going to Bethlehem. (795)

The Blessed Mother

I am reliving these moments
with Our Lady. With great longing,
I am waiting for the Lord's coming.
Great are my desires.
I desire that all humankind
come to know the Lord.
I would like to prepare all nations
for the coming of the Word Incarnate.
(793)

Holy Communion

Of myself I can do nothing,
but when you sustain me,
all difficulties are nothing for me …
I fear the day when I do not receive
Holy Communion.
This Bread of the Strong
gives me all the strength I need
to carry on my mission
and the courage to do
whatever the Lord asks of me. (91)

HOLY COMMUNION

O Jesus, I want to bring souls
to the fount of your mercy
to draw the reviving water of life
with the vessel of trust …
**My child, that you may answer
my call worthily,
receive me daily in Holy Communion.
It will give you strength … (1489)**

Holy Communion

I often feel God's presence
after Holy Communion
in a special and tangible way.
I know God is in my heart …
I do not lose the presence of God
in my soul,
and I am closely united with him.
With him I go to work,
with him I go to recreation,
with him I suffer, with him I rejoice …
(318)

Holy Communion

Once after Holy Communion,
I heard these words:
You are our dwelling place.
At that moment, I felt in my soul
the presence of the Holy Trinity,
the Father, the Son and the Holy Spirit.
I felt that I was the temple of God.
I felt I was a child of the Father.
I cannot explain all this,
but the spirit understands it well. (451)

Holy Communion

My heart is a living tabernacle
in which the living Host is reserved.
I have never sought God
in some far-off place, but within myself.
It is in the depths of my own being
that I commune with my God. (1302)

HOLINESS

O my Jesus,
how very easy it is to become holy;
all that is needed is a bit of good will.
If Jesus sees this little bit of good will
in the soul,
he hurries to give himself to the soul,
and nothing can stop him …
absolutely nothing. (291)

Holiness

… nothing can discourage a soul who is holy. (1333)

Sanctity

Great are the faults
committed by the tongue.
The soul will not attain sanctity
if it does not keep watch over its tongue.

(92)

CONSCIENCE

O most gracious Lord,
how merciful it is on your part
to judge each one
according to his conscience
and his discernment,
and not according to people's talk.
My spirit delights and feeds
more and more on your wisdom … (1456)

CONSCIENCE

Oh, if souls would only be willing
to listen, at least a little,
to the voice of conscience and the voice
– that is, the inspirations –
of the Holy Spirit!
I say 'at least a little' because
once we open ourselves
to the influence of the Holy Spirit,
he himself will fulfil what is lacking in us.

(359)

The Present Moment

It is a great thing to know
how to make use of the present moment.
(296)

The Present Moment

O Jesus, I want to live
in the present moment,
to live as if this were
the last day of my life.
I want to use every moment scrupulously
for the greater glory of God …
I want to look upon everything
from the point of view
that nothing happens
without the will of God. (1183)

ONLY ONE TASK

Jesus, I have only one task
to carry out in my lifetime,
in death, and throughout eternity,
and that is to adore
your incomprehensible mercy. (1553)

TRANSFORMATION

I must be on my guard, especially today,
because I am becoming over-sensitive
to everything.
Things I would not pay any attention to
when I am healthy bother me today …
O my Jesus, transform me into yourself
by the power of your love,
that I may be a worthy tool
in proclaiming your mercy. (783)

Reconciliation

The Lord said to me:

… Tell souls … to look for solace … in the Tribunal of Mercy. There the greatest miracles take place [and] are incessantly repeated. To avail oneself of this miracle … it suffices to come with faith to the feet of my representative and to reveal to him one's misery … The miracle of Divine Mercy restores that soul in full.

(1446-1448)

RECONCILIATION

One thing alone is necessary:
that the sinner set ajar
the door of his heart, be it ever so little,
to let in a ray of God's merciful grace,
and then God will do the rest. (1507)

Forgiveness

We resemble God most
when we forgive our neighbours.
God is love, goodness, and mercy …
(1148)

Confession

Today the Lord said to me:
When you approach the confessional,
know this,
that I myself am waiting there for you.
I am only hidden by the priest,
but I myself act in your soul. (1602)

OCEAN OF MERCY

Jesus, I trust in you;
I trust in the ocean of your mercy.
You are a mother to me. (249)

OCEAN OF MERCY

O Uncreated Beauty,
whoever comes to know you once
cannot love anything else.
I can feel the bottomless abyss of my soul,
and nothing will fill it but God himself.
I feel that I am drowned in him
like a single grain of sand
in a bottomless ocean. (343)

OCEAN OF MERCY

O incomprehensible God!
I am aware that I am dissolving in you
like a drop in an ocean.
I am aware that you are within me
and all about me,
that you are in all things
that surround me,
in all that happens to me. (478)

THE HOLY SPIRIT

My heart has been accustomed
to the inspirations of the Holy Spirit,
to whom I am faithful. (1504)

Suffering for You

O Christ, suffering for you
is the delight of my heart and my soul …
I will glorify you in abandonment
and darkness, in agony and fear,
in pain and bitterness, in anguish of spirit
and grief of heart.
In all things may you be blessed. (1662)

FEAR NOT

… the soul should not be too fearful, because God will never test us beyond what we are able to bear. (106)

Fear Not

Since I came to love God
with my whole being
and with all the strength of my heart,
fear has left me …
I have come to know him well.
God is love, and his Spirit is peace …
I have placed my trust in God
and fear nothing. (589)

Fear Not

… praise the Lord's mercy
by trusting in his mercy all your life
and especially at the hour of your death.
And fear nothing … whoever you are;
the greater the sinner,
the greater his right to your mercy,
O Lord. (598)

At the hour of death

I realise more and more
how much every soul needs
God's mercy throughout life
and particularly at the hour of death.
(1036)

At the hour of death

Oh, how much we should pray
for the dying!
Let us take advantage of mercy
while there is still time for mercy. (1035)

At the last hour

When I went for adoration,
I heard these words:
… at the hour of death … a soul has nothing with which to defend itself except my mercy. Happy is the soul that during its lifetime immersed itself in the Fountain of Mercy, because justice will have no hold on it.
(1074-1075)

Union with the Dying

My union with the dying
is still as close as ever.
Oh, how incomprehensible is God's mercy
that the Lord allows me,
by my unworthy prayer,
to come to the aid of the dying.
I try to be at the side
of every dying person whenever I can.
Have confidence in God, for … his mercy
surpasses our understanding. (880)

The Constancy of God

Do with me as you please, Lord,
only give me the grace
to be able to love you
in every event and circumstance …
I trust in you, Jesus,
for you are unchangeable.
My moods change,
but you are always the same, full of mercy.

(1489)

The Constancy of God

You, my Lord God, cannot change.
You are always the same.
Heaven can change,
as well as everything that is created;
but you, Lord, are ever the same
and will endure forever …
Father of infinite mercy, I, your child,
wait longingly for your coming. (854)

THE CONSTANCY OF GOD

[God] gave me to understand
how fleeting all earthly things are,
and [how] everything that appears great
disappears like smoke, and does not give
the soul freedom but weariness.
Happy the soul that understands these
things and with only one foot
touches the earth. (1141)

TEMPTATION

People have often sown doubt in my soul,
and I myself have sometimes become
frightened at the thought that I was,
after all, an ignorant person
and did not have knowledge
of many things,
above all, spiritual things. (121)

TEMPTATION

Today after Holy Communion, Jesus [said]:
Temptation gives you a chance to show me your fidelity. (1560)

Envy

I have experienced
how much envy there is,
even in religious life.
I see that there are few truly great souls,
ready to trample on everything
that is not God …
Oh, how fragile is the foundation
of those who elevate themselves
at the expense of others! What a loss!
(833)

PRAYER

There are times in life
when the soul finds comfort
only in profound prayer.
Would that souls knew
how to persevere in prayer at such times.
This is very important. (860)

Prayer

Patience, prayer and silence –
these are what give strength to the soul.
There are moments when one should be
silent, and when it would be inappropriate
to talk with creatures …
At such times, I live solely by faith and
when I feel strengthened by God's grace,
then I am more courageous in speaking
and communicating with my neighbours.
(944)

Prayer

… I heard the words:
You will save more souls through prayer and suffering than will a missionary through his teachings and sermons alone. I want to see you as a sacrifice of living love, which only then carries weight before me. (1756-1767)

Prayer

… I prayed continuously,
asking Jesus to strengthen me
and to grant me the power
of his Holy Spirit
that I might carry out his holy will
in all things,
because from the beginning
I have been aware of my weakness. (56)

A ROYAL CHILD

I am going forward through life
amidst rainbows and storms,
but with my head held high with pride,
for I am a royal child.
I feel that the blood of Jesus
is circulating in my veins,
and I have put my trust in the great mercy
of the Lord. (992)

Holy Trinity

Most Holy Trinity,
I trust in your infinite mercy.
God is my Father and so I, his child,
have every claim to his divine heart;
and the greater the darkness,
the more complete our trust should be.

(357)

Permeated by God

Permeated by God to its very depths
[my soul] drowns in his beauty;
it completely dissolves in him
– I am at a loss to describe this …
These moments are short,
but their effects are lasting. (767)

As a wild flower

I want to live pure as a wild flower;
I want my love always to be turned to you,
just as a flower
that is always turning to the sun. (306)

Thanksgiving

I desire that my whole life be
but one act of thanksgiving to you,
O God … (1285)

Thanksgiving

I spent the whole day in thanksgiving
and gratitude kept flooding my soul.
O my God, how good you are,
how great is your mercy! (1661)

God's Choice

God usually chooses the weakest and simplest souls as tools for his greatest works; that we can see that this is an undeniable truth when we look at the men he chose to be his apostles; or again, when we look at the history of the church and see what great works were done by souls that were the least capable of accomplishing them ... (464)

Lost in God

O my Jesus, you are the life of my life …
O God … how great you are!
I found my destiny at the moment
when my soul lost itself in you,
the only object of my love.
In comparison with you,
everything is nothing. (57)

For all eternity

From the very first time
that I came to know the Lord,
the gaze of my soul became drowned
in him for all eternity. (231)

ETERNITY

There are mysteries
that the human mind will never fathom
here on earth;
eternity will reveal them. (1656)

Pure Love of God

The Lord, so very gentle though he is,
delights in humble souls.
I have come to know that
only love is of any value;
love is greatness;
nothing, no works, can compare
with a single act of pure love of God.
(1092)

An Ardent Love of God

An ardent love of God
sees all around itself
constant opportunities to share itself
through deed, word, and prayer. (1313)

So loved by God

What a paradise it is for a soul
when the heart knows itself
to be so loved by God ... (1756)

THE SACRED HEART

I saw the Sacred Heart of Jesus in the sky,
in the midst of a great brilliance.
The rays were issuing from the wound
[in his side] and spreading out
over the entire world. (1796)

THE SPIRIT OF MERCY

If we live in the spirit of mercy,
we ourselves will obtain mercy. (550)